Chefs' Special

South Indian Kitchen

Chefs' Special

South Indian Kitchen

Kalp Mithal: Executive Chef, The Park, New Delhi

Lustre Press
Roli Books

Acknowledgements

I would like to thank Arun Mathur, who helped me cook and style the dishes for photography, and without whose dedication this book would not have seen the light of day.

I am grateful to Park Hotel for providing me with the means of fulfilling my creative pursuits.

Last, but not least, I would like to thank my publisher and Arti Walia for their efforts in putting the book together – and, of course, my guru, Shri Sai Baba.

Dedication

To the two ladies in my life: my wife, Sangeeta, and my daughter, Ananya.

Flavours of South India

It was not long ago that any reference to south Indian food would bring to the mind of a north Indian images of *dosas* (plain pancakes), *vadas* (fried patties), *idlis* (steamed rice cakes) and *uttapams* (vegetable pancakes). But the fact is that the cuisine of all the four south Indian states, Andhra Pradesh, Tamil Nadu, Karnataka and Kerala, is not exactly the same.

South Indian cooking uses methods of steaming and dry roasting of masalas. Very little oil is used in its cooking, as a result, the food tends to be lighter and simpler compared to the food eaten in the north. Today south Indian food is very popular all over India.

Rice is the staple food in the south. From plain boiled rice to *idlis* to crisp *appams* (pancakes), rice-based dishes are eaten in all possible forms. Rice is served with *rasam* (thin soup) and *sambhar* (red gram with vegetables). To prepare these two dishes, red gram is boiled in plenty of water till it is soft. The upper part, which is mainly water, is strained in different ways to make different kinds of *rasams*. The lower part, which is thick, is used to make *sambhar* by adding vegetables and seasonings. Rice is also served with dry and curried vegetables, meats, seafood, and curd preparations like *pacheda*.

Karnataka has four distinct regions – Mangalore, Karvar or Konkan, Bidar and Bangalore. Special mention must be made of the small town of Bagde which produces crimson red Bagde chillies, full of flavour, but not very hot. The curries and *sambhars* of this region are reddish in colour, but not spicy compared to the food in other south Indian states. The food is rustic and hearty in Bidar, in north Karnataka, and the cuisine of the Saraswat brahmins of Mangalore is delicate and subtle.

Several dishes from Kerala mentioned in this book are from the Moplah Muslims of the Malabar region of Kerala. Moplahs are descendants of Arab traders who came to trade, settled down and married local women. Their cuisine has a great deal in common with food all over Kerala in its excessive use of coconut and coconut oil and its dependence on rice. Arab influence is evident in some of the dishes such as *alisa* (wheat soup with meat) and *biryani* (rich flavoured meat rice). On the eve of weddings, *neichork* (clarified butter rice) is served and in the morning *kanji* (rice soup) is served.

In a Tamil Nadu wedding, dishes like *poriyal* (dry mixed vegetables) and *avial* (mixed vegetables) with steamed rice and *semiya payasam* (vermicelli pudding) for dessert are usually served.

On occasions like childbirth, *bhajiyas* (red gram patties), *medu vadas* (black gram patties) and *thengai saadham* (coconut rice) are served. Pongal is the largest festival, celebrating the harvesting of the new crop. *Ven pongal* (rice pongal) is offered to the gods and then distributed. A south Indian meal is rounded off with an after-dinner *paan* (betel leaf), containing spices, which aid digestion, such as aniseed, cloves, areca nut and cardamom.

South Indian cuisine is not difficult to cook. Crisp, tangy, nutritious, spicy and wholesome – take 100 gm of adventurous spirit, deep-fry in 10 tbsp of enthusiasm, season with a pinch of experimentation and create your own south Indian gourmet delight!

Basic Preparations

Gun Powder: Take 100 gm split black gram (*urad dal*), 50 gm whole red chillies (*sabut lal mirch*), 5 gm mustard seeds (*rai*), 3 gm asafoetida (*hing*), 20 gm curry leaves (*kadhi patta*), 3 gm lime concentrate and salt to taste.

In a wok (*kadhai*), dry roast the split black gram on a slow fire for 5-8 minutes. Keep aside. Dry roast the whole red chillies and the mustard seeds, separately. Add all the ingredients together and grind to a fine powder. Store in an airtight jar. Serve with clarified butter.

Sambhar Powder: Take 75 gm whole red chillies (*sabut lal mirch*), 15 ml oil, 200 gm coriander seeds (*sabut dhaniya*), 50 gm cumin seeds (*sabut jeera*), 20 gm fenugreek seeds (*methi dana*), 20 gm black peppercorns (*sabut kali mirch*), 20 gm mustard seeds (*rai*), 20 gm Bengal gram (*chana dal*), 20 gm red gram (*arhar dal*), 20 gm poppy seeds (*khuskhus*), 2 cinnamon (*dalchini*) sticks, 5 curry leaves (*kadhi patta*) and 20 gm turmeric (*haldi*) powder.

Fry the whole red chillies in oil. Dry roast all the other ingredients (except turmeric powder) separately till they release a strong aroma. Grind all the ingredients including turmeric powder together to a fine powder. Store the powder in an airtight container and use when required.

Garam Masala Powder: Take 2 cloves (*laung*), 2 green cardamoms (*choti elaichi*), 1 cinnamon (*dalchini*) stick, 1 bay leaf (*tej patta*), 5 black peppercorns (*sabut kali mirch*). Grind all these spices together to a fine powder. Sieve and then store in an airtight jar. For maximum flavour, make small quantities at a time, since it loses its aroma if kept for too long.

Coconut (*nariyal*) Chutney: Take 5 coconuts (*nariyal*), grated; 15 gm ginger (*adrak*), chopped; 6 green chillies, deseeded; 50 gm Bengal gram (*chana dal*), roasted; 15 ml oil; 5 gm mustard seeds (*rai*); 15 gm green gram (*moong dal*), 6 whole red chillies (*sabut lal mirch*) and a few curry leaves.

Grind the coconuts with a little water, ginger and green chillies to make a smooth paste. Add the Bengal gram to the paste. Heat the oil in a wok (*kadhai*); add the mustard seeds. When they start to crackle, add the green gram and fry till golden brown. Add the whole red chillies and curry leaves.

Pour this in the coconut paste and check for seasoning. Serve cold with *idlis*, *dosas*, *vadas*, etc.

Tomato Chutney: Take 2 kg tomatoes, washed, quartered; 1 kg onions, peeled, quartered; 200 ml oil; 15 whole red chillies (*sabut lal mirch*); 5 gm mustard seeds (*rai*); 20 gm split black gram (*urad dal*); 10 sprigs curry leaves (*kadhi patta*) and salt to taste.

Heat a little in a wok (*kadhai*); add the onions and fry for 8-10 minutes till translucent. Add the whole red chillies and tomatoes. Cook for 15-20 minutes. Remove from the flame. When the mixture cools, grind to a fine paste. Heat 1 tbsp oil in the same wok; add the mustard seeds, split black gram and curry leaves. Sauté for a few minutes. Add this to the paste and check for seasoning. Serve cold.

Coconut (nariyal) Milk: Take 1 coconut (nariyal), grated and 600 ml of hot water.

Blend the coconut with 200 ml of hot water for 8-10 minutes in a blender. Strain the coconut mixture through a muslin cloth. This is the first extract.

Repeat the same procedure with the remaining coconut and 200 ml of water. Strain again to get the second extract.

Repeat again with 200 ml of water. This is the third extract.

If refrigerated, the coconut milk can stay for up to 3-4 days.

Tamarind (imli) Extract: To make tamarind extract, take 200 gm of dry tamarind and soak in 400 ml of hot water for half an hour. Then squeeze the juice through a strainer and discard the pulp. Use this extract for any recipe you want.

Clarified Butter (ghee): Heat some unsalted butter until it melts and froths. Remove the foam that rises on the top. Pour the melted butter into a heat-proof container. Discard the milk solids that are left behind. Let it cool at room temperature and then chill. When the chilled fat rises to the top, spoon it off, leaving the clarified butter behind.

Ginger-garlic (*adrak-lasan*) Paste: Take equal amounts of ginger and garlic and soak overnight. Peel, chop and process in an electric blender with a small quantity of water. Blend at a high speed to make a smooth paste. Remove and store in an airtight container and keep in the refrigerator for later use. The paste will keep for up to 4-6 weeks.

Yoghurt (*dahi*): If you want to set yoghurt at home buy some starter (culture) from a sweet (*mithai*) shop.

Heat 1 lt milk till it is warm to touch. Add 2 tsp of the starter to it and stir well. Transfer the mixture to a clay pot, cover with a lid and then keep in a warm place to allow it to set. In winter, it usually takes longer to set and also needs to be kept warmer than usual. In the summer months, it sets in a relatively short time.

Buttermilk (*matha*): Take 50 gm sour yoghurt and add 150 ml water. Blend together.

Alisa
Wheat soup with meat

Preparation time: 20 min.
Cooking time: 30 min.
Serves: 2-4

Ingredients:

Broken wheat (*dalia*)	1 cup / 200 gm
Chicken or mutton, diced	1¼ cups / 250 gm
Onion, large, diced	1
Cinnamon (*dalchini*) stick	1
Salt to taste	
Water	4 cups / 800 ml
Clarified butter (*ghee*)	2 tbsp / 30 gm
Madras onion, chopped	1 tbsp / 15 gm
Sugar	a pinch

Method:

1. Cook the broken wheat with the chicken or mutton, onion, cinnamon stick, salt and water for 20-25 minutes.
2. When the meat is cooked, remove from the fire and mash it well with a wooden spoon. Keep aside.
3. Heat the clarified butter (keep aside 1 tsp for garnishing) in a heavy-bottomed pan; add the Madras onion and fry till light golden brown. Add the soup and check for seasoning.
4. Serve hot with a dash of clarified butter and a pinch of sugar.

Thakkali Rasam
Tomato soup

Preparation time: 15 min.
Cooking time: 30-40 min.
Serves: 2-4

Ingredients:

Tomatoes, large, chopped	4
Red gram (*arhar dal*), soaked for 5 minutes	4 tsp / 20 gm
Salt to taste	
Green chillies	4
Ginger (*adrak*), chopped	1 tsp / 5 gm
Turmeric (*haldi*) powder	¼ tsp / 1½ gm
Water	3 cups / 600 ml
Green coriander (*hara dhaniya*), chopped	1 tsp / 5 gm

For the tempering:

Clarified butter (*ghee*)	2 tsp / 10 gm
Mustard seeds (*rai*)	¾ tsp
Cumin seeds (*sabut jeera*)	¾ tsp
Whole red chillies (*sabut lal mirch*), broken	2
Asafoetida (*hing*)	¼ tsp / 1½ gm
Curry leaves (*kadhi patta*)	a few

Method:

1. In a deep pot, add the tomatoes, red gram, salt, green chillies, ginger, turmeric powder, water and green coriander and cook for 30-35 minutes. Mash well with a wooden spoon till all the ingredients are well mixed. Keep aside.

2. Heat the clarified butter in a pan. Add all the ingredients for the tempering. Cook for a few seconds only.

3. Pour this over the soup. Check for seasoning. Serve hot.

Kanji
Rice soup flavoured with coconut milk

Preparation time: 30 min.
Cooking time: 10 min.
Serves: 4-5

Ingredients:

Broken rice, washed,
drained — 1¼ cups / 250 gm
Water — 5 cups / 1 lt
Coconut (*nariyal*) milk,
extract (see p. 10) — ¾ cup / 150 ml
Salt to taste

Method:

1. Cook the broken rice in a pot with water till it is very soft. Keep aside.
2. Pour in the coconut milk and check for seasoning.
3. Serve hot.

Hot Dip
To soak rice at short notice,
use hot water instead of cold water.

Mutton Samosas
Mutton patties

Preparation time: 1 hr.
Cooking time: 40-45 min.
Serves: 2-4

Ingredients:

Mutton, minced	1 cup / 200 gm
Refined flour (*maida*)	½ cup / 100 gm
Salt	½ tsp / 3 gm
Oil	¼ cup / 50 ml
Onion, big, chopped	1
Ginger-garlic (*adrak-lasan*) paste	1 tsp / 5 gm
Turmeric (*haldi*) powder	a pinch
Coriander (*dhaniya*) powder	1 tsp / 5 gm
Garam masala (see p. 9)	a pinch
Green chillies, chopped	1 tbsp / 15 gm
Green coriander (*hara dhaniya*), chopped	½ bunch
Oil for frying	

Method:

1. Sieve the refined flour with salt and knead with enough water to make a hard dough. Cover the dough with a moist cloth.
2. Heat the oil in a pan. Add the onion and ginger-garlic paste, sauté for a minute. Add the remaining ingredients except the oil. Cook till the mutton is done. Remove from the flame. Keep aside.
3. Divide the dough into lemon-sized balls. Roll each ball into 4"-diameter discs. Place 1 tbsp of mutton mixture in half of the disc. Fold the other half over, enclosing the filling. Pinch the edges to seal.
4. Heat the oil in a wok (*kadhai*); deep-fry the patties till golden brown. Serve hot with tomato sauce.

Murukku
Rice curls

Preparation time: 2 hrs.
Cooking time: 30 min.
Serves: 4

Ingredients:

Rice, soaked for 2 hours,
   drained, dried   1 cup / 200 gm
Coconut (*nariyal*) milk,
   extract (see p. 10)   1 cup / 200 ml
Salt to taste
Black cumin seeds (*shahi jeera*)   1 tsp / 5 gm
Oil for frying

Method:

1. Powder, sieve and roast the rice flour. Cool and keep aside.
2. Heat the coconut milk extract in a pan; add the roasted rice flour, salt and black cumin seeds. Mix well.
3. Remove the rice flour mixture from the flame and keep aside to cool. Knead the mixture with water and make a fairly stiff dough.
4. Divide the dough into lemon-sized balls and shape them into rings.
5. Heat the oil in a wok (*kadhai*) and deep-fry the rings till crisp.
6. Cool and store in airtight containers.

Medu Vada
Black gram patties

Preparation time: 6 hrs.
Cooking time: 30 min.
Serves: 4-6 (makes 8-10)

Ingredients:

Split black gram (*urad dal*),
   soaked for 6 hours   ¼ cup / 50 gm
Green coriander (*hara dhaniya*),
   chopped   2 tbsp / 30 gm
Cumin seeds (*sabut jeera*)   1 tbsp / 15 gm
Salt to taste
Green chillies, chopped   4
Oil for frying

Method:

1. Drain the split black gram and grind till very smooth. Make a thick batter with a little water.
2. Add the green coriander, cumin seeds, salt and green chillies. Mix well. Divide the batter into equal portions. Wet your palm, take a portion and make a patty with a hole in the centre. Make similar patties till all the batter is used up.
3. Heat the oil on a slow fire; release the patties gently into the oil and deep-fry till golden brown and crisp. Remove with a slotted spoon, and drain on absorbent kitchen towels.
4. Serve hot.

Sago Vada
Sago patties

Preparation time: 45 min.
Cooking time: 30-45 min.
Serves: 2-4 (makes 8-10)

Ingredients:

Sago (*sabu dana*)	½ cup / 100 gm
Buttermilk (*matha*) (see p. 11)	½ cup / 100 ml
Gram flour (*besan*)	½ cup / 100 gm
Red chilli powder	1 tsp / 5 gm
Asafoetida (*hing*)	a pinch
Green chillies, chopped	2
Green coriander (*hara dhaniya*), chopped	1 tsp / 5 gm
Clarified butter (*ghee*)	1 tsp / 5 gm
Salt to taste	
Oil for frying	

Method:

1. Soak the sago in buttermilk for 30 minutes.
2. Add all the ingredients (except oil) to the soaked sago. Season with salt and add enough water to make a stiff batter.
3. Divide the sago batter into equal portions and shape each portion into round patties.
4. Heat the oil in a wok (*kadhai*); add a few patties at a time and deep-fry for 15-20 minutes or till golden brown. Remove with a slotted spoon, and drain on absorbent kitchen towels.
5. Serve hot with coconut chutney (see p. 9).

Chilli Effect
To make hardened asafoetida soft,
add a green chilli to it.

Bhajiya
Red gram patties

Preparation time: 2 hrs.
Cooking time: 20 min.
Serves: 4-6 (makes 15-20)

Ingredients:

Red gram (*arhar dal*), washed,
soaked for 2 hours   1 cup / 200 gm
Onions, medium, chopped   2
Coriander leaves (*hara dhaniya*),
chopped   3 tbsp / 45 gm
Curry leaves (*kadhi patta*)   20
Green chillies, chopped   3
Garlic (*lasan*) cloves, crushed   5
Salt to taste
Oil for frying

Method:

1. Drain the red gram and grind coarsely. Add all the ingredients (except oil) and a little water to make a stiff batter.
2. Divide the batter into equal portions and shape the portions into patties.
3. Heat the oil in a wok (*kadhai*); add a few patties at a time and deep-fry till golden brown. Remove with a slotted spoon, and drain on absorbent kitchen towels.
4. Serve hot with coconut and tomato chutneys (see p. 9).

Arvi Bonda
Crispy colocasia

Preparation time: 1 hr.
Cooking time: 45-50 min.
Serves: 2-4

Ingredients:

Colocasia (*arvi*), boiled, mashed	500 gm
Green chillies, chopped	6
Yoghurt (*dahi*)	1 tbsp / 15 gm
Ginger (*adrak*), chopped	1 tsp / 5 gm
Asafoetida (*hing*)	a pinch
Green coriander (*hara dhaniya*), chopped	1 tsp / 5 gm
Salt to taste	

For the batter:

Refined flour (*maida*)	1 cup / 200 gm
Gram flour (*besan*)	½ cup / 100 gm
Rice flour	½ cup / 100 gm
Baking soda	a pinch

Oil for frying

Method:

1. In a bowl, mix the colocasia with green chillies, yoghurt, ginger, asafoetida and green coriander thoroughly. Season with salt and shape the mixture into medium-sized balls.
2. Combine all the ingredients of the batter and add enough water to make a batter of semi-thick consistency.
3. Heat the oil in a wok (*kadhai*); dip the colocasia balls into the batter and then, carefully, lower them into the wok in small batches.
4. Cook on a medium flame until crisp; remove with a slotted spoon and drain on absorbent kitchen towels. Serve hot.

Quick Setting

Yoghurt which has not set properly, if placed in a covered dish in the sun for some time will set immediately.

Achhar Idli
Pickled pancakes

Preparation time: 2½ hrs.
Cooking time: 25 min.
Serves: 4-6 (makes 30)

Ingredients:

Split black gram (*urad dal*),
   soaked for 2 hours   2½ cups / 500 gm
Semolina (*suji*), soaked
   for 20 minutes   2 cups / 400 gm
Fenugreek seeds (*methi dana*)   1 tsp / 5 gm
Mixed pickle, chopped   ¼ cup / 50 gm
Salt to taste

Method:

1. Drain the split black gram and grind to a fine paste by adding a little water.
2. Drain the semolina and grind with the fenugreek seeds.
3. Mix the two pastes and add enough water to make a batter of dropping consistency. Season with salt.
4. Take the idli moulds. Pour 1 tbsp of the batter in each mould, put some mixed pickle over it and then top with another tbsp of the batter.
5. Steam for 20 minutes.
6. Serve hot with gun powder (see p. 8) and coconut chutney (see p. 9).

Sevain Idli

Vermicelli pancakes

Preparation time: 2½ hrs.
Cooking time: 30 min.
Serves: 6-8 (makes 20)

Ingredients:

Split black gram (*urad dal*),
   soaked for 2 hours   1 cup / 200 gm
Semolina (*suji*), soaked for
   20 minutes   1 cup / 200 gm
Fenugreek seeds (*methi dana*)   1 tsp / 5 gm
Vermicelli (*sevain*), soaked for
   20 minutes   2 cups / 400 gm
Salt to taste

Method:

1. Drain the split black gram and grind to a fine paste by adding a little water.
2. Drain the semolina and grind with the fenugreek seeds.
3. Mix the two pastes together; add the drained vermicelli and season with salt.
4. Take the idli moulds; pour 1 tbsp of the batter in each mould and steam for 20 minutes.
5. Serve hot with coconut and tomato chutneys (see p. 9).

Masala Uttapam
Spicy pancakes

Preparation time: 1 hr.
Cooking time: 25 min.
Serves: 2-4 (makes 8-10)

Ingredients:

Rice	¾ cup / 150 gm
Split black gram (*urad dal*)	¾ cup / 150 gm
Salt to taste	

For the filling:

Oil	¼ cup / 50 ml
Onion, large, finely chopped	1
Tomatoes, large, finely chopped	2
Green chillies, finely chopped	4
Cumin seeds (*sabut jeera*)	1 tsp / 5 gm
Green coriander (*hara dhaniya*), finely chopped	2 tbsp / 30 gm

Method:

1. Prepare the batter by grinding together rice, split black gram, a little water and salt. Keep aside.
2. Heat a little oil in a pan; add the onion, tomatoes, green chillies, cumin seeds, green coriander and salt to taste. Mix thoroughly and cook for a few minutes. Keep the filling aside.
3. Heat a non-stick pan; pour a ladleful of the batter and spread it evenly. Cook over a medium heat.
4. Spread the filling on the batter, sprinkle a little oil around the sides and cook until the pancake is brown on the underside. Turn and cook the other side as well. Repeat till all the batter is used up.
5. Serve hot with coconut and tomato chutneys (see p. 9).

Plain Dosa
Plain pancakes

Preparation time: 4½ hrs.
Cooking time: 20 min.
Serves: 2-4 (makes 8-10)

Ingredients:

Rice, soaked for 4 hours	¾ cup / 150 gm
Split black gram (*urad dal*) soaked for 4 hours	¼ cup / 50 gm
Salt to taste	
Oil	4 tbsp / 60 ml

Method:

1. Drain the rice and split black gram and grind them together, adding enough water to make a smooth batter. Stir in the salt. Keep aside.
2. In a non-stick pan, pour a ladleful of the batter and spread it evenly to make a paper-thin pancake. Sprinkle some oil over the pancake and cook till golden brown. Make similar pancakes till all the batter is used up.
3. Fold them as desired.
4. Serve hot with coconut chutney (see p. 9), gun powder (see p. 8) and *araitha sambhar* (see p. 64).

Masala Dosa
Stuffed pancakes

Preparation time: 4½ hrs.
Cooking time: 30 min.
Serves: 2-4 (makes 8-10)

Ingredients:

Rice, soaked for 4 hours	¾ cup / 150 gm
Split black gram (*urad dal*), soaked for 4 hours	¼ cup / 50 gm
Salt to taste	

For the filling:

Oil	2 tbsp / 30 ml
Onion, large, sliced	1
Mustard seeds (*rai*)	1 tsp / 5 gm
Split green gram (*moong dal*)	1 tbsp / 15 gm
Bengal gram (*chana dal*)	1 tbsp / 15 gm
Whole red chillies (*sabut lal mirch*)	2
Cashew nuts (*kaju*)	4 tsp / 20 gm
Curry leaves (*kadhi patta*)	a few
Potatoes, boiled, mashed	2
Turmeric (*haldi*) powder	1 tsp / 5 gm

Method:

1. Drain rice and split black gram. Grind together. Add salt and a little water to make a smooth batter.
2. Heat the oil in a pan; add the onion and sauté till translucent. Add the mustard seeds, split green gram, Bengal gram and sauté for 3-4 minutes. Add the whole red chillies, cashew nuts, curry leaves, potatoes and turmeric powder. Cook for 3-4 minutes more. Keep the filling aside.
3. In a non-stick pan, pour a ladleful of the batter and spread it evenly. Sprinkle a little oil around the sides and cook till golden brown. Put the filling in the centre of the pancake and fold as desired.
4. Serve hot with coconut chutney (see p. 9) and *araitha sambhar* (see p. 64).

Adai
Mixed dal pancakes

Preparation time: 2½ hrs.
Cooking time: 20 min.
Serves: 2-4 (makes 10-15)

Ingredients:

Split black gram (*urad dal*)	½ cup / 100 gm
Lentil (*masoor dal*)	½ cup / 100 gm
Bengal gram (*chana dal*)	½ cup / 100 gm
Rice	1 cup / 100 gm
Whole red chillies (*sabut lal mirch*)	6
Onions, chopped	¼ cup / 50 gm
Salt to taste	
Coconut (*nariyal*), grated	4 tbsp / 60 gm
Asafoetida (*hing*)	½ tsp / 3 gm
Green coriander (*hara dhaniya*), chopped	2 tbsp / 30 gm
Oil	2 tbsp / 30 ml

Method:

1. Clean and soak the first four ingredients in 4 cups of water with the whole red chillies for 2 hours. Then drain and grind these ingredients coarsely with onions, salt, coconut, asafoetida and green coriander.

2. Add enough water to the above mixture to make a batter of dropping consistency.

3. Heat the griddle (*tawa*); pour a ladleful of the batter, spread it evenly to make a paper-thin pancake. Sprinkle a little oil around the sides and cook until golden brown on the underside. Fold as desired. Make similar pancakes till all the batter is used up.

4. Serve hot with jaggery.

Okra Magic

If you run short of split black gram (urad dal), *while making* dosas *or* idlis, *add okra* (bhindi) *which has been ground to a paste. The* dosas *will turn crisp.*

Godumai
Wheat flour pancakes

Preparation time: 1½ hrs.
Cooking time: 1 hr.
Serves: 4-6 (makes 10-15)

Ingredients:

Wholewheat flour (*atta*)	2 cups / 400 gm
Rice flour	1 cup / 200 gm
Buttermilk (*matha*) (see p. 11)	½ cup / 100 ml
Salt to taste	
Green chillies, finely chopped	2

For the tempering:

Oil	½ tbsp / 8 ml
Mustard seeds (*rai*)	¼ tsp / 1½ gm
Cumin seeds (*sabut jeera*)	½ tsp / 3 gm
Curry leaves (*kadhi patta*)	a few
Green coriander (*hara dhaniya*), chopped	1 tsp / 5 gm

Method:

1. In a large bowl, mix the wholewheat and rice flours with the buttermilk, salt and green chillies. Add enough water to the mixture to make a batter of dropping consistency. Let it ferment for 1 hour.
2. Heat the oil in a pan; add the mustard seeds, cumin seeds and curry leaves. Fry till the seeds start sputtering. Add the green coriander. Pour this tempering into the batter.
3. Heat a non-stick pan. Pour a ladleful of the batter and spread it evenly to make a paper-thin pancake. Sprinkle a little oil around the sides and cook until golden brown.
4. Serve hot with coconut chutney (see p. 9).

Leaf it!
Left over batter of idlis *and* dosas
will not turn sour, if you put a
betel leaf on top of the batter.

Erachi Khorma
Mutton korma

Preparation time: I hr.
Cooking time: I hr. 15 min.
Serves: 1-2

Lamb

Ingredients:

Mutton, cut, in pieces	225 gm
Oil	2½ tbsp / 40 ml
Cinnamon (*dalchini*) sticks	3
Cloves (*laung*)	3
Green cardamoms (*choti elaichi*)	4
Onions, medium, finely sliced	2
Green chillies, ground	3
Ginger (*adrak*), ground, 1" piece	1
Garlic (*lasan*) cloves, ground	7
Coriander (*dhaniya*) powder	1 tsp / 5 gm
Red chilli powder	1 tsp / 5 gm
Turmeric (*haldi*) powder	¼ tsp / 1½ gm
Yoghurt (*dahi*)	½ cup / 100 ml
Tomatoes, small, chopped	2
Salt to taste	
Water	1½ cups / 300 ml
Coconut (*nariyal*), grated	1 cup / 200 gm
Aniseed (*saunf*)	2 tsp / 10 gm
Poppy seeds (*khuskhus*)	1 tsp / 5 gm

Method:

1. Heat the oil in a deep pan; add all the ingredients till turmeric powders. Fry for a few minutes. Stir in the mutton. Reduce the heat and cook covered, stirring occasionally. Add the next four ingredients and cook till the mutton is tender.

2. Make a paste of the remaining ingredients and add to the pan. Let the mutton mixture simmer for a while and then remove from the flame. Serve hot.

Erachi Ulathiatu

Fried mutton flavoured with coconut

Preparation time: 1 hr.
Cooking time: 1 hr.
Serves: 2-3

Ingredients:

Mutton, boneless, cut into ½" pieces	500 gm
Coconut (*nariyal*) oil	½ cup / 100 ml
Coconut (*nariyal*), pieces	½
Turmeric (*haldi*) powder	¼ tsp / 1½ gm

Roast and powder:

Coriander seeds (*sabut dhaniya*)	2 tbsp / 30 gm
Whole red chillies (*sabut lal mirch*)	10
Cinnamon (*dalchini*) sticks	3
Cloves (*laung*)	6
Black peppercorns (*sabut kali mirch*)	8

Madras onions, sliced	12
Ginger (*adrak*), sliced, ½" piece	1
Curry leaves (*kadhi patta*)	15
Salt to taste	

Method:

1. Heat 2 tbsp coconut oil in a wok (*kadhai*); add the pieces of coconut and turmeric powder. Sauté for a while and keep aside.
2. Mix the mutton with the roasted, powdered spices, the Madras onions, ginger, curry leaves and salt in a wok.
3. Add enough water to cook the mutton dry.
4. Bring the mutton mixture to a boil. Cover and simmer till the mutton is tender and dry.
5. Heat the remaining coconut oil; add the cooked mutton and fry well.
6. Garnish with fried pieces of coconut and serve hot with steamed rice and *araitha sambhar* (see p. 64).

Erachi Porichathu
Fried mutton

Preparation time: I hr.
Cooking time: I hr.
Serves: 2-4

Ingredients:

Mutton, boneless pieces	250 gm
Aniseed (*saunf*)	2 tsp / 10 gm
Garlic (*lasan*), pod	1
Salt to taste	
Turmeric (*haldi*) powder	a pinch
Red chilli powder	2 tsp / 10 gm
Water	2 cups / 400 ml
Oil for frying	

Method:

1. Grind the aniseed, garlic and salt to a smooth paste. Marinate the mutton with the paste for half an hour. Keep aside.
2. In a non-stick pan, cook the mutton, turmeric and red chilli powders on a slow fire for 45 minutes or till the water is completely absorbed and the mutton is tender. Keep aside.
3. Heat the oil in the wok (*kadhai*); deep-fry the mutton till golden brown.
4. Serve hot.

Lamb

Safety Salt
Salt sprinkled into a frying pan will prevent the oil from splashing or food from sticking to the bottom.

Eralu Achhar
Pickled liver

Preparation time: 45 min.
Cooking time: 30 min.
Serves: 2-4

Lamb

Ingredients:

Liver, cubed	1½ cups / 300 gm
Salt to taste	
Red chilli powder	1 tsp / 5 gm
Lemon (*nimbu*) juice	2 tbsp / 30 ml
Oil for tempering	
Mustard seeds (*rai*)	1 tsp / 5 gm

Method:

1. Boil the liver with a little salt; when fully cooked, drain and discard the water. Keep aside.
2. Marinate the liver cubes with salt, red chilli powder and lemon juice for half an hour.
3. Heat the oil in a pan; add the mustard seeds and when it crackles stir in the marinated liver. Mix well and keep aside.
4. Tastes best after 6-8 hours.

Refrigerating Meat
Meat kept as one large portion
in the freezer will keep for a
longer time than minced or
chopped meat.

Erachi Varatiyathu

Spicy mutton masala

Preparation time: 1 hr.15 min.
Cooking time: 1 hr.
Serves: 2-4

Ingredients:

Mutton	250 gm
Oil	2 tbsp / 30 ml
Onions, big, sliced	3
Grind to a paste:	
Green chillies	4
Ginger (*adrak*)	1 tsp / 5 gm
Garlic (*lasan*), pod	1
Aniseed (*saunf*)	1 tsp / 5 gm
Coriander (*dhaniya*) powder	2 tsp / 10 gm
Red chilli powder	1 tsp / 5 gm
Garam masala (see p. 9)	1 tsp / 5 gm
Turmeric (*haldi*) powder	¼ tsp / 1½ gm
Salt to taste	
Tomatoes, chopped	2
Sugar	1 tsp / 5 gm
Lemon (*nimbu*) juice	1
Green coriander (*hara dhaniya*), chopped	2 tbsp / 30 gm

Method:

1. Heat the oil in a pan. Add the onions, green chilli paste, red chilli powder, garam masala and turmeric powder. Fry well.
2. Add the mutton and fry till the oil separates. Add enough water to cook the mutton and have a thick gravy.
3. When the mutton ¾ th done, add salt, tomatoes, sugar and lemon juice. Cook till the mutton is tender. Serve hot, garnished with green coriander.

Malabar Kozhambu
Malabar chicken curry

Preparation time: I hr.
Cooking time: **45 min.**
Serves: **2-4**

I n g r e d i e n t s :

Chicken, cleaned, cut into pieces	500 gm
Oil	1½ tbsp / 25 ml
Cinnamon (*dalchini*) stick, 2"	1
Cloves (*laung*)	6
Green cardamoms (*choti elaichi*)	6
Onion, sliced	1
Green chillies, slit	3
Ginger (*adrak*), sliced	a small piece

Roast and grind with vinegar:

Coriander seeds (*sabut dhaniya*)	3 tsp / 15 gm
Whole red chillies (*sabut lal mirch*)	10
Turmeric (*haldi*) powder	¼ tsp / 1½ gm
Garlic (*lasan*) cloves	6
Vinegar (*sirka*)	1 tbsp / 15 ml

Coconut (*nariyal*), grated,milk extracted 3 times (see p. 10)	1
Potatoes, diced	1¼ cups / 250 gm
Salt to taste	

For the tempering:

Oil	1 tsp / 5 ml
Onion, chopped	1
Mustard seeds (*rai*)	1 tsp / 5 gm
Curry leaves (*kadhi patta*)	10

Method:

1. Heat the oil in a wok (*kadhai*); add the cinnamon stick, cloves, green cardamoms, onion, green chillies and ginger. Cook till the onion turns translucent.
2. Add the ground spices and stir-fry for a few minutes. Add the chicken and the third extract of the coconut milk.
3. When the chicken is half cooked, add the potatoes and the second extract of the coconut milk and let it simmer.
4. When the chicken is tender, add the first extract of the coconut milk and salt. Mix well.
5. For the tempering, heat the oil in a pan. Add the onion and when it browns add the mustard seeds and curry leaves. Sauté for a few seconds and pour this into the chicken curry. Mix well.
6. Serve hot with steamed rice.

Fridge Fresh
Coriander leaves will stay garden fresh,
if you store them in an airtight
container in the refrigerator.

Kozi Porichathu
Fried chicken

Preparation time: 40 min.
Cooking time: 40 min.
Serves: 3-4

Ingredients:

Chicken, pieces	800 gm
Oil	4 tbsp / 60 ml
Cinnamon (*dalchini*) sticks	2
Aniseed (*saunf*)	2 tsp / 10 gm
Garlic (*lasan*) cloves, chopped	2 tbsp / 30 gm
Madras onions, chopped	1¼ cups / 250 gm
Tomatoes, medium, chopped	4
Turmeric (*haldi*) powder	½ tsp / 3 gm
Red chilli powder	2½ tsp / 15 gm
Water	¼ cup / 50 ml
Salt to taste	
Coconut (*nariyal*), grated	1
Ginger (*adrak*), julienned	½ tsp / 3 gm

Method:

1. Heat the oil in a wok (*kadhai*); add the cinnamon sticks, aniseed and garlic. Sauté for a few seconds.
2. Add the Madras onions, tomatoes and the chicken. Sauté for 10 minutes.
3. Add the turmeric powder, red chilli powder, water and salt; mix well.
4. Cook the chicken till ¾th done. Add the coconut and ginger and cook till the chicken is tender.
5. Serve hot.

Tomato Therapy

Tomatoes that have become overripe and soft, can be salvaged by soaking them in a bowl of salt water for half an hour.

Kozi Khorma

Chicken flavoured with coconut

Preparation time: 30 min.
Cooking time: 40 min.
Serves: 4-6

Ingredients:

Chicken, pieces	1 kg
Oil	4½ tbsp / 70 ml
Ginger (*adrak*), chopped	1 tsp / 5 gm
Garlic (*lasan*), chopped	1 tsp / 5 gm
Coconut (*nariyal*), grated	½
Green chillies, chopped	10
Poppy seeds (*khuskhus*)	1½ tsp / 8 gm
Bengal gram (*chana dal*)	1½ tsp / 8 gm
Aniseed (*saunf*)	1½ tsp / 8 gm
Star anise (*chakri phool*)	1
Cloves (*laung*)	3
Cinnamon (*dalchini*) stick	1
Curry leaves (*kadhi patta*)	15
Onions, sliced	¾ cup / 150 gm
Tomatoes, chopped	½ cup / 100 gm

Method:

1. Heat 1 tsp of oil in a wok (*kadhai*); add the ginger, garlic, coconut and green chillies. Stir-fry for a while. Keep aside.

2. Dry roast the poppy seeds, Bengal gram, aniseed and star anise. Grind to a paste with a little water.

3. Heat the remaining oil in a separate wok. Add the cloves, cinnamon stick, curry leaves and onions. Sauté till the onions turn light golden brown.

4. Add the chicken and the poppy seed paste and mix for 5 minutes.

5. Now add a little water and the tomatoes. Cook for 10-15 minutes. Check for seasoning.

6. Serve hot with steamed rice.

Chicken

Meen Porichathu
Fried fish

Preparation time: 1hr.
Cooking time: 30 min.
Serves: 2-4

Ingredients:

Fish, cut into pieces, cleaned	250 gm
Red chilli powder	2 tsp / 10 gm
Turmeric (*haldi*) powder	½ tsp / 3 gm
Aniseed (*saunf*)	½ tsp / 3 gm
Garlic (*lasan*) cloves	4
Cinnamon (*dalchini*) stick, 3 cm	1
Cloves (*laung*)	2
Lemon (*nimbu*) juice	½
Salt to taste	
Oil for frying	

Method:

1. Combine all the ingredients (except the fish and oil) and grind to a smooth paste.
2. Marinate the fish with this paste and keep aside for 1 hour.
3. Heat the oil in a pan and shallow-fry the fish for 2-3 minutes on both sides till golden brown.
4. Serve hot.

Meen Mulaki Hathu

Fried chilli fish

Preparation time: 45 min.
Cooking time: 30 min.
Serves: 3-4

Ingredients:

Fish, medium-sized, cleaned	4
Coconut (*nariyal*) oil	1 tbsp / 10 ml
Mustard seeds (*rai*)	½ tsp / 3 gm
Fenugreek seeds (*methi dana*)	1 tsp / 5 gm
Onions, medium, chopped	4
Green chillies, chopped	3
Garlic (*lasan*) cloves, crushed	6
Red chilli powder	1½ tsp / 8 gm
Turmeric (*haldi*) powder	½ tsp / 3 gm
Tamarind (*imli*), extract (see p. 10)	25 gm
Curry leaves (*kadhi patta*)	20
Salt to taste	
Tomatoes, chopped	2

Method:

1. Heat the coconut oil in a wok (*kadhai*); add the mustard and fenugreek seeds. When they start to crackle add the onions, green chillies and garlic. Fry for a few seconds, and then add the red chilli and turmeric powders. Mix well for a minute.
2. Add the tamarind juice and let the mixture simmer for some time.
3. Add the fish, curry leaves, salt and tomatoes. Cook covered for 10 minutes or till the fish is done.
4. Serve hot with steamed rice.

Meen Molee
Fish curry

Preparation time: 45 min.
Cooking time: 25-30 min.
Serves: 2-4

Ingredients:

Fish, pieces, cleaned	500 gm
Coconut (*nariyal*), piece	1
Turmeric (*haldi*) powder	½ tsp / 3 gm
Green chillies, slit	8
Ginger (*adrak*), chopped	2 tsp / 10 gm
Garlic (*lasan*) cloves	4
Cashew nuts (*kaju*)	5
Coconut (*nariyal*) oil	2 tbsp / 30 ml
Onion, medium, sliced	1
Tomato, large, quartered	1
Coconut (*nariyal*) milk, first extract (see p. 10)	2 cups / 400 ml
Cumin (*jeera*) powder	1 tsp / 5 gm
Salt to taste	

Method:

1. Pat dry the fish and keep it aside.
2. Grind together the coconut, turmeric powder, 6 green chillies, ginger, garlic and cashew nuts to a smooth paste.
3. Heat the coconut oil; add the onion and the remaining green chillies. Sauté for a while. Add the coconut paste and a little water.
4. Add the tomato, coconut milk and the fish. Sprinkle cumin powder and simmer till the fish is cooked. Check for seasoning.
5. Serve hot.

Fresher Fish

*To make refrigerated fish taste like
fresh fish, defrost the fish, add
½ tbsp salt and juice of ½ lemon.
Keep aside for an hour.
Rinse and cook.*

Era Kozhambu

Prawn curry

Preparation time: 45 min.
Cooking time: 30 min.
Serves: 2-4

Ingredients:

Prawns (*jhinga*), medium	500 gm
Oil	½ cup / 100 ml
Curry leaves (*kadhi patta*)	20
Mustard seeds (*rai*)	½ tsp / 3 gm
Ginger (*adrak*), paste	2 tsp / 10 gm
Garlic (*lasan*) cloves, paste	4
Onions, chopped	½ cup / 100 gm

Grind to a paste:

Whole red chillies (*sabut lal mirch*)	4
Coriander seeds (*sabut dhaniya*)	3 tsp / 15 gm
Turmeric (*haldi*) powder	½ tsp / 3 gm

Tomatoes, chopped	½ cup / 100 gm
Tamarind (*imli*), extract (see p. 10)	2 tbsp / 30 gm
Salt to taste	
Coconut (*nariyal*), grated	½

Method:

1. Heat the oil in a wok (*kadhai*); add the curry leaves (keep aside a few for garnishing), mustard seeds, ginger-garlic paste and onions. Sauté for a while.
2. Add the ground paste. Cook for 5 minutes. Mix the tomatoes, tamarind pulp and salt.
3. Stir the prawns in; after the first boil simmer for 10-12 minutes or till the prawns are cooked.
4. Heat a little oil in another pan; fry the remaining curry leaves for 3-4 seconds.
5. Serve hot, garnished with coconut and the fried curry leaves.

Grave Gravy
*Don't thicken a curry with
cornflour or gram flour and
ruin its taste. Use more coconut
milk or coconut paste and
see the difference.*

Araitha Sambhar
Red gram with vegetables

Preparation time: 45 min.
Cooking time: 45 min.
Serves: 2-4

Ingredients:

Red gram (*arhar dal*), soaked for 5 minutes	½ cup / 100 gm
Madras onions, chopped	¼ cup / 50 gm
Turmeric (*haldi*) powder	½ tsp / 3 gm
Salt to taste	
Brinjals (*baingan*), diced	¼ cup / 50 gm
Capsicum (*Shimla mirch*), diced	½
Drumstick (*saijan ki phali*), diced	1
Potato, medium, diced	1

Grind to a paste:

Oil	2 tsp / 10 ml
Coconut (*nariyal*), grated	3 tbsp / 45 gm
Whole red chillies (*sabut lal mirch*)	2
Fenugreek seeds (*methi dana*)	¾ tsp

(See photograph on front cover)

Asafoetida (*hing*)	½ tsp / 3 gm
Coriander seeds (*sabut dhaniya*)	2½ tsp / 15 gm
Bengal gram (*chana dal*)	2 tsp / 10 gm
Cumin seeds (*sabut jeera*)	¾ tsp
Tamarind (*imli*), extract (see p. 10)	½ tsp / 3 gm

For the tempering:

Oil	1 tsp / 5 ml
Mustard seeds (*rai*)	¾ tsp
Cumin seeds (*sabut jeera*)	½ tsp / 3 gm
Aniseed (*saunf*)	½ tsp / 3 gm
Whole red chillies (*sabut lal mirch*)	2
Curry leaves (*kadhi patta*)	a few
Salt to taste	
Green coriander (*hara dhaniya*), chopped	2 tbsp / 30 gm

M e t h o d :

1. Boil the red gram, Madras onions, turmeric powder and salt in 2 cups of water. Keep aside.
2. Steam the brinjals, capsicum, drumstick and potato. Keep aside.
3. Grind all the ingredients mentioned to a fine paste.
4. Add the steamed vegetables to the red gram mixture and cook for 10-12 minutes. Add the ground paste and the tamarind extract and cook for 5 minutes more on a low heat.
5. For the tempering, heat the oil in a wok; add the mustard seeds, cumin seeds, aniseed, whole red chillies and curry leaves. Fry for a few seconds and then pour this into the above mixture. Add salt.
6. Serve hot, garnished with green coriander.

Boil it
Don't boil vegetables in cold water.
Always use boiling water for better results.

Parangi Kai Puli Curry

Tangy pumpkin curry

Preparation time: 30 min.
Cooking time: 25-30 min.
Serves: 4-6

Ingredients:

Red pumpkin (*lal kaddu*), skinned, cut into 1½" cubes	2½ cups / 500 gm
Oil	2 tbsp / 30 ml
Madras onions, sliced	4 tbsp / 60 gm
Garlic (*lasan*) cloves, finely chopped	15
Coriander (*dhaniya*) powder	1 tsp / 5 gm
Red chilli powder	1 tsp / 5 gm
Turmeric (*haldi*) powder	¼ tsp / 1½ gm
Salt to taste	
Tamarind (*imli*), extract (see p. 10)	¼ tsp / 1½ gm
Tomatoes, quartered	2
Jaggery (*gur*)	2 tsp / 10 gm
Aniseed (*saunf*)	½ tsp / 3 gm

Method:

1. Heat the oil in a wok (*kadhai*); sauté the Madras onions and garlic for a few minutes.
2. Add the coriander powder, red chilli powder, turmeric powder, salt and the red pumpkin. Sauté for 5 minutes.
3. Add the tamarind extract, tomatoes and 1½ cups of water. Cover and cook for 10 minutes or till the red pumpkin is half done.
4. Add the jaggery and aniseed. Cook for 12-15 minutes more. Simmer till the vegetable is completely cooked.
5. Serve hot.

Avial
Mixed vegetables with coconut

Preparation time: 1hr.
Cooking time: 40-50 min.
Serves: 2-4

Ingredients:

Carrots, peeled, cut 2" long	120 gm
Drumsticks (*saijan ki phali*), cut 2" long	120 gm
White pumpkin (*safed kaddu*), cut 2" long	120 gm
Raw bananas, cut 2" long	120 gm
Beans, cut 2" long	120 gm
Yam (*jimikand*), cut 2" long	120 gm
Snake gourd (*lauki*), cut 2" long	120 gm
Salt to taste	
Turmeric (*haldi*) powder	¼ tsp / 1½ gm
Coconut (*nariyal*), grated	8 tbsp / 120 gm
Green chillies	6-8
Cumin seeds (*sabut jeera*)	1 tsp / 5 gm
Yoghurt (*dahi*)	1 cup / 200 gm
Curry leaves (*kadhi patta*)	a few
Coconut (*nariyal*) oil	¼ cup / 50 ml

Method:

1. Boil all the vegetables in a pot with water, salt and turmeric powder for 10-12 minutes. Drain the water and keep the vegetables aside.
2. Grind together more than half of the coconut, green chillies and cumin seeds into a paste.
3. Add the yoghurt and curry leaves to the coconut paste and mix well.
4. Add this yoghurt mixture to the boiled vegetables and cook till it starts boiling. Pour the coconut oil, mix well and remove from the fire.
5. Serve hot, garnished with the remaining coconut.

Vegetarian

Selecting Beans

When buying beans, ensure that they are firm, crisp, tender and snap readily when broken. Pods in which seeds are immature are best.

Mottacos Poriyal

Stir-fried cabbage

Preparation time: 40 min.
Cooking time: 20-25 min.
Serves: 2-4

Ingredients:

Cabbage, finely shredded, washed,	2½ cups / 500 gm
Coconut (*nariyal*) oil	3 tbsp / 45 ml
Mustard seeds (*rai*)	½ tsp / 3 gm
Onions, chopped	4½ tbsp / 70 gm
Green chillies, chopped	3
Curry leaves (*kadhi patta*)	a few
Split black gram (*urad dal*)	½ tsp / 3 gm

Grind to a paste:

Cumin seeds (*sabut jeera*)	½ tsp / 3 gm
Aniseed (*saunf*)	½ tsp / 3 gm
Black peppercorns (*sabut kali mirch*)	5
Garlic (*lasan*) cloves	5
Coconut (*nariyal*), grated	¼
Salt to taste	

Method:

1. Heat the coconut oil in a steel pan. Add the mustard seeds, onions, green chillies, curry leaves and split black gram. Sauté till the black gram turns light golden brown.

2. Add the cabbage and the cumin seed paste. Stir well. Mix half the grated coconut and check for seasoning. Cover and cook on a slow flame for 12-15 minutes.

3. Serve hot, garnished with the remaining coconut.

Vegetarian

Gutti Vonkaya Kura

Stuffed brinjals

Preparation time: 45 min.
Cooking time: 30-35 min.
Serves: 2-4

Ingredients:

Brinjals (*baingan*), small, round,
    whole   8
Coriander seeds (*sabut dhaniya*) 1½ tsp / 8 gm
Salt to taste
Whole red chillies (*sabut lal mirch*)   3
Coconut (*nariyal*), grated   1 tbsp / 15 gm
Onion, chopped   1
Oil   2 tsp / 10 ml
Turmeric (*haldi*) powder   a pinch
Tamarind (*imli*), extract
    (see p. 10)   4 tsp / 20 gm

Method:

1. Slit the brinjals into 4 sections. Keeping the top portion intact. Fry the brinjals and keep aside.
2. Coarsely grind the coriander seeds, salt, whole red chillies, coconut and onion.
3. Heat the oil in a pan; add the turmeric powder and the coarsely ground ingredients. Fry for a few minutes. Add the tamarind extract and cook till the water dries up. Keep the filling aside to cool.
4. Stuff the brinjals with this filling carefully.
5. In a pan, gently place the stuffed brinjals and cook covered for 10-12 minutes on a slow fire.
6. Serve hot.

Vegetarian

Yelamincha Saadham
Lemon rice

Preparation time: 30 min.
Cooking time: 30 min.
Serves: 4-6

Ingredients:

Rice, soaked for 10 minutes	2½ cups / 500 gm
Aniseed (*saunf*)	1 tsp / 5 gm
Turmeric (*haldi*) powder	1 tsp / 5 gm
Split black gram (*urad dal*)	3 tsp / 15 gm
Coconut (*nariyal*) oil	2 tbsp / 30 ml
Cashew nuts (*kaju*)	2 tbsp / 30 gm
Peanuts (*moongphalli*)	2 tbsp / 30 gm
For the tempering:	
Mustard seeds (*rai*)	½ tsp / 3 gm
Curry leaves (*kadhi patta*)	20
Whole red chillies (*sabut lal mirch*)	5
Bengal gram (*chana dal*)	3 tsp / 15 gm
Asafoetida (*hing*)	a pinch
Lemon (*nimbu*) juice	3
Salt to taste	

Method:

1. Boil 5 cups of water in a pot; add the rice and cook till done. Drain and keep aside.
2. Roast and powder the aniseed, turmeric powder and split black gram. Add this mixture to the cooked rice and mix well.
3. Heat the coconut oil in a pan; fry the cashew nuts and peanuts. Keep aside.
4. In the same oil, add the mustard seeds, curry leaves, whole red chillies, Bengal gram and asafoetida. Sauté till light golden brown.
5. Add this tempering to the rice and mix well. Add the lemon juice and nuts. Check for seasoning.
6. Serve hot with coconut chutney (see p. 9).

Thayir Saadham
Yoghurt rice

Preparation time: 15 min.
Cooking time: 15 min.
Serves: 2-4

Ingredients:

Rice, soaked for 8 minutes	1½ cups / 300 gm
For the tempering:	
Oil	2 tbsp / 30 ml
Mustard seeds (*rai*)	1 tsp / 5 gm
Asafoetida (*hing*)	a pinch
Curry leaves (*kadhi patta*)	10
Green chillies, chopped	2 tsp / 10 gm
Ginger (*adrak*), chopped	2 tsp / 10 gm
Yoghurt (*dahi*)	3 cups / 600 gm
Salt to taste	

Method:

1. Boil 3 cups of water in a pot. Add the rice and cook till done. Drain and keep aside.
2. For the tempering, heat the oil in a pan; add the mustard seeds, asafoetida, curry leaves, green chillies and ginger. Sauté for 2 minutes. Keep aside.
3. Take a big bowl; mix the rice, yoghurt and salt.
4. Pour the tempering over the rice mixture and mix.
5. Serve with pickle.

Thengai Saadham

Coconut rice

Preparation time: 30 min.
Cooking time:15 min.
Serves: 3-4

Ingredients:

Rice, washed	2¼ cups / 450 gm
For the tempering:	
Coconut (*nariyal*) oil	1 tbsp / 15 ml
Mustard seeds	½ tsp / 3 gm
Bengal gram (*chana dal*)	½ tsp / 3 gm
Split black gram (*urad dal*)	½ tsp / 3 gm
Cumin seeds (*sabut jeera*)	¼ tsp / 1½ gm
Asafoetida (*hing*)	a pinch
Curry leaves (*kadhi patta*)	a few
Sesame seeds (*til*), roasted, powdered	1 tbsp / 15 gm
Coconut (*nariyal*), grated	3 tbsp / 45 gm
Green chillies, chopped	1 tsp / 5 gm
Ginger (*adrak*), chopped	1 tsp / 5 gm
Salt to taste	
Cashew nuts (*kaju*), fried	12

Method:

1. Boil 4½ cups of water in a pot. Add the rice and cook till done. Drain and keep aside.
2. For the tempering, heat the coconut oil in a wok (*kadhai*); add the mustard seeds and when they crackle add the Bengal gram, split black gram and cumin seeds. Fry for 2-3 seconds.
3. Add the remaining ingredients (keep 1 tbsp of coconut aside for garnishing) and cook for a few minutes.
4. In a bowl, mix the rice with the above mixture.
5. Serve hot, garnished with grated coconut.

Kadugu Saadham
Mustard rice

Preparation time: 30 min.
Cooking time: 15 min.
Serves: 3-4

Ingredients:

Rice, washed	2¼ cups / 450 gm
Grind to a paste:	
Mustard seeds (*rai*)	2 tbsp / 30 gm
Green chillies, chopped	8
Onion, medium	½
Coconut (*nariyal*), piece	3 tbsp / 45 gm
Ginger (*adrak*)	1 tsp / 5 gm
Garlic (*lasan*)	½ tsp / 3 gm
Turmeric (*haldi*) powder	1 tsp / 5 gm
Tamarind (*imli*), extract	
(see p. 10)	2 tbsp / 30 gm
For the tempering:	
Coconut (*nariyal*) oil	2 tbsp / 30 ml
Mustard seeds (*rai*)	½ tsp / 3 gm
Split black gram (*urad dal*)	1 tsp / 5 gm
Bengal gram (*chana dal*)	1 tsp / 5 gm
Whole red chillies (*sabut lal mirch*)	8
Curry leaves (*kadhi patta*)	a few
Salt to taste	

Method:

1. Cook the rice in 4½ cups of salted water. Drain and add the ground mustard seed paste. Mix well.

2. For the tempering, heat the coconut oil in a wok (*kadhai*); add the mustard seeds. When they begin to crackle, add the split black gram, Bengal gram and whole red chillies. Fry till light golden brown. Add the curry leaves and salt.

3. In a big bowl, mix the rice and the tempering with a flat spoon. Serve hot.

Eruchina Kay Pachhadi

Groundnut chutney

Preparation time: 45 min.
Cooking time: 15 min.

Ingredients:

Groundnuts (*moongphalli*), roasted	¾ cup / 150 gm
Green chillies	8
Coconut (*nariyal*), fresh, grated	¼
Oil	2 tsp / 10 ml
Mustard seeds (*rai*)	½ tsp / 3 gm
Split black gram (*urad dal*)	1 tsp / 5 gm
Curry leaves (*kadhi patta*)	10
Tamarind (*imli*), extract (see p.10)	1 tbsp / 15 gm
Salt to taste	

Method:

1. Grind the groundnut, green chillies and coconut together. Keep aside.
2. Heat the oil in a pan; add the mustard seeds. When they crackle, add the split black gram and fry till golden brown.
3. Add the curry leaves, groundnut paste, tamarind extract and check for seasoning. Cook for 2-3 minutes over a medium flame.
4. Remove from the flame, cool and then store in an airtight jar and refrigerate.

(*See photograph on page 81, **centre***)

Vonkya Pachhadi

Brinjal chutney

Preparation time: 30 min.
Cooking time: 45 min.

Ingredients:

Brinjals (*baingan*), boiled, mashed	500 gm
Oil	5 tsp / 25 ml
Green chillies	15
Coconut (*nariyal*), grated	3 tbsp / 45 gm
Turmeric (*haldi*) powder	½ tsp / 3 gm
Tamarind (*imli*), extract	
(see p. 10)	1 tbsp / 15 gm
Salt to taste	
Mustard seeds (*rai*)	¼ tsp / 1½ gm
Curry leaves (*kadhi patta*)	12

Method:

1. Heat 2 tsp of oil in a wok (*kadhai*); fry the green chillies till golden brown. Remove the green chillies and keep aside.
2. In the same oil, sauté the mashed brinjals till brown. Keep aside.
3. Pound the green chillies, coconut and turmeric to a fine powder.
4. Add this powder to the brinjal, with the tamarind extract and salt. Mix well.
5. Heat the remaining oil; sauté the mustard seeds and curry leaves for a few seconds. Pour this over the brinjal mixture and serve.

*(See photograph on page 81, **left**)*

Kariyapak Pachhadi
Curry leaves chutney

Ingredients:

Curry leaves (*kadhi patta*), washed, dried	1¼ cups / 250 gm
Green chillies	20
Oil	2 tsp / 10 ml
Bengal gram (*chana dal*)	1 tsp / 5 gm
Mustard seeds (*rai*)	½ tsp / 3 gm
Lemon (*nimbu*) juice	1
Salt to taste	

Method:

1. Grind the curry leaves and green chillies to a smooth paste.
2. Heat the oil in a pan; add the Bengal gram and mustard seeds and sauté till they crackle.
3. Remove from the flame and add the paste. Mix well. Add the lemon juice and check for seasoning.
4. Cool and transfer to an airtight jar. Serve as an accompaniment with plain *idlis* or steamed rice.

*(See photograph on page 81, **right**)*

Mirialu and Eligadda Podi

Garlic and coconut powder

Ingredients:

Whole red chillies (*sabut lal mirch*)	4
Black peppercorns (*sabut kali mirch*)	1 tbsp / 15 gm
Coconut (*nariyal*), grated	½
Salt to taste	
Turmeric (*haldi*) powder	a pinch
Oil	2 tsp / 10 ml
Mustard seeds (*rai*)	1 tsp / 5 gm
Curry leaves (*kadhi patta*)	8
Garlic (*lasan*), ground	½ cup / 100 gm

Method:

1. Dry roast the whole red chillies, black peppercorns and coconut for 3-5 minutes.
2. Add the salt and turmeric powder and roast for another 2 minutes.
3. Heat the oil in a pan; add the mustard seeds. When they crackle, add the curry leaves and garlic. Fry for 6-8 seconds.
4. Add the dry roasted ingredients and fry further for 3-4 minutes. Remove the pan from the heat and cool. Grind all the ingredients into a powder.
5. Serve with rice.

(*See photograph on page 85, **left***)

Chitlam Podi
Mixed dal powder

Preparation time: 20 min.
Cooking time: 15 min.

Ingredients:

Whole red chillies (*sabut lal mirch*)	30 gm
Coconut (*nariyal*), fresh, grated	4 tsp / 20 gm
Salt to taste	
Tamarind (*imli*), extract (see p. 10)	1 tbsp / 15 gm
Bengal gram (*chana dal*)	2 tbsp / 30 gm
Green gram (*moong dal*)	2 tbsp / 30 gm
Split black gram (*urad dal*)	2 tbsp / 30 gm
Sugar	1 tsp / 5 gm
Clarified butter (*ghee*)	2 tsp / 10 gm
Curry leaves (*kadhi patta*)	12-15

*(See photograph on page 85, **right**)*

Method:

1. Dry roast the whole red chillies and coconut for 3-5 minutes. Keep aside to cool.
2. Grind the above mixture with salt and tamarind extract. Keep aside.
3. Roast the Bengal gram, green gram and split black gram on a very low flame, till golden brown. When cool grind to a fine powder.
4. Mix the two powders together with the sugar.
5. Heat the clarified butter in a pan; add the curry leaves and the powder mixture. Fry lightly for a minute and then remove from the flame.
6. Cool and store in an airtight jar.

Parippu Payasam
Green gram flavoured with coconut milk

Preparation time: 45 min.
Cooking time: 40-50 min.
Serves: 6-8

Ingredients:

Split green gram (*moong dal*) 2¼ cups / 250 gm
Coconut (*nariyal*) milk,
   second extract (see p.10)   2 cups / 400 ml
Jaggery (*gur*), broken   3 cups / 600 gm
Coconut (*nariyal*) milk,
   first extract (see p.10)   1¼ cups / 250 ml
Green cardamom
   (*choti elaichi*) powder   ½ tsp / 3 gm
Raisins (*kishmish*), fried   ¼ cup / 50 gm
Cashew nuts (*kaju*), fried   ¼ cup / 50 gm
Clarified butter (*ghee*)   5 tbsp / 75 gm

Method:

1. In a wok (*kadhai*); roast the split green gram to a light brown colour.
2. Pour in the second extract of the coconut milk and cook till the split green gram turns very soft.
3. Add the jaggery and cook till a thick consistency is obtained.
4. Now pour the first extract of the coconut milk and cook on a slow fire. Add the green cardamom powder and mix well. Remove from the fire.
5. Serve hot, garnished with raisins, cashew nuts and clarified butter.

Desserts

Yel Adai

Coconut and rice pancakes

Preparation time: 20 min.
Cooking time: 20 min.
Serves: 2-4

Ingredients:

Rice, washed, soaked for
  10-15 minutes   2½ cups / 500 gm
Water   2½ cups / 500 ml
Jaggery (*gur*)   1¼ cups / 250 gm
Coconut (*nariyal*), grated   1¼ cups / 250 gm
Clarified butter (*ghee*)   ¾ cup / 150 gm
Salt to taste
Green cardamom
  (*choti elaichi*), seeds   1 tsp / 5 gm
Banana leaves, cut into 4″ squares   4

Method:

1. To prepare the jaggery syrup, boil the water, add the jaggery and stir well. Remove the scum from time to time. Cook till the syrup is reduced to ¼th.
2. Add the coconut and cook for 5-8 minutes more. Stir in the clarified butter reserving about 25 gm.
3. Grind the rice with enough water to make a batter of dropping consistency. Add the salt and green cardamom seeds.
4. Smear the remaining clarified butter over the banana leaves. Place them over hot plates so that the leaves become soft. Pour the rice batter over the banana leaves, spread the jaggery mixture and fold in the shape of an envelope. Steam them for 18-20 minutes. Serve hot or cold.

Rawa Kesari

Semolina flavoured with saffron

Preparation time: 40 min.
Cooking time: 25-30 min.
Serves: 6-8

Ingredients:

Semolina (*suji*), sieved	1¼ cups / 250 gm
Clarified butter (*ghee*)	1¼ cups / 250 gm
Saffron (*kesar*), soaked in lukewarm water	a few strands
Water	3¼ cups / 650 ml
Sugar	2½ cups / 500 gm
Green cardamom (*choti elaichi*) powder	1 tsp / 5 gm
Raisins (*kishmish*), fried	¼ cup / 50 gm
Cashew nuts (*kaju*), fried	¼ cup / 50 gm

Method:

1. Heat 50 gm of clarified butter in a pan. Add the semolina and fry for 10-12 minutes or till golden brown.
2. Add the saffron with the water and sugar. Cook till the water evaporates.
3. Add the remaining clarified butter and fry till the semolina mixture leaves the sides. Mix the green cardamom powder.
4. Serve hot, garnished with raisins and cashew nuts.

Suggested Menus

Non-vegetarian
Meen Molee (*Fish curry*)
Erachi Porichathu (*Fried mutton*)

or

Vegetarian
Gutti Vonkya Kura (*Stuffed brinjals*)
Mottacos Poriyal (*Stir-fried cabbage*)

Accompaniments
Yelamincha Saadham (*Lemon rice*)
Kariyapak Pachhadi (*Curry leaves chutney*)

Dessert
Rawa Kesari (*Semolina flavoured with saffron*)

Non-vegetarian
Era Kozhambu (*Prawn curry*)
Kozi Porichathu (*Fried chicken*)

or

Vegetarian
Avial (*Mixed vegetables with coconut*)
Parangi Kai Puli Curry (*Tangy pumpkin curry*)

Accompaniments
Kadugu Saadham (*Mustard rice*)
Eruchina Kay Pachhadi (*Groundnut chutney*)

Dessert
Parippu Payasam (*Green gram flavoured with coconut milk*)

Glossary of Cooking Terms

Batter	—	A mixture of flour, liquid and sometimes other ingredients, of a thin or thick, creamy consistency.
Dry roast	—	To roast the spices on a griddle (*tawa*) without any oil or clarified butter.
Marinate	—	To soak meat, fish or vegetable in a mixture of seasoning ingredients to add flavour and to make it tender.
Purée	—	To press food through a fine sieve or blend in a blender to a smooth, thick mixture.
Sauté	—	Fry or cook quickly in a little oil over a high flame.
Simmer	—	To keep boiling or bubbling gently on a low flame.
Steam	—	To cook food in steam. Generally food to be steamed is put in a perforated container which is placed over a pan of boiling water.
Stir-fry	—	To cook with a little oil stirring briskly and continuously.
Temper	—	Combine spices and flavourings with hot oil or clarified butter, and then pour this over the main preparation.

Index

ACCOMPANIMENTS

Rice

Chutneys and Powders

DESSERTS

ISBN: 81-7436-157-X

Third impression 2004
© **Roli & Janssen BV 2001**
Published in India by Roli Books
in arrangement with Roli & Janssen
M-75 Greater Kailash II (Market)
New Delhi 110 048, India
Ph: ++91 (011) 29212271, 29212782, 29210886
Fax: ++91 (011) 29217185, E-mail: roli@vsnl.com
Website: rolibooks.com

Photographs: Dheeraj Paul

Printed and bound in Singapore